Ward Off the Night

poems by

Leslie Clark

Finishing Line Press
Georgetown, Kentucky

Ward Off the Night

ACKNOWLEDGMENTS

"Edges", "Our Wilderness" and "Plunge" were previously published in
slightly different versions in *Mirage* literary and arts magazine..

"The Movement of Cows" was previously published in *The Poet's Domain,*
volume 15.

"Battles in the Night" was previously published in *The Poet's Domain*, volume
19.

Publisher: Leah Maines
Editor: Christen Kincaid
Cover Art: Chrissy Teachout
Author Photo: Tracy Starall
Cover Design: Elizabeth Maines McCleavy

Printed in the USA on acid-free paper.
Order online: www.finishinglinepress.com
          also available on amazon.com

Author inquiries and mail orders:
Finishing Line Press
P. O. Box 1626
Georgetown, Kentucky 40324
U. S. A.

Table of Contents

For my writing friends all over this country.

BEES

For three days, they hang from the patio ceiling, a black globe lamp,
hundreds of them, clumping, roiling, a chain-saw buzz.
The swarm sends scouts for miles to search out a perfect nest-place.
Small patrols whizz by our ears like rifle bullets.
We can't tell if they're "killers." They wear their harmless
honeybee masks well, hanging there, a portentous presence.
We research by modem—sites tell us they're at a docile
stage while searching for a nest—no home turf to protect.
Nevertheless, we take no chances, avoid the backyard. The dog
goes for walks out front. We try to co-exist in peace.
We don't want them dead—just gone.

A friend tells of her bee-swarming experience, how they crawled
under her door, through electrical outlets, a relentless black tide.
She had to call the man with killing chemicals—it was her or them.
For days she heard the plipping of bodies inside the walls,
stepped on husks of bees as crisp as cocoa puffs.

Our more cooperative swarm finally departs, arcing
through the air like a cannonball. The last scouting expedition
returns to find they've vanished—no breadcrumb trail to follow.
They cluster in the spot vacated by the mother group,
a small dark teardrop. They gather no pollen, feed no queen.
Their purpose gone, they drop to the concrete patio floor
one by one.

SUMMER CROWS

On the roof, crows are attacking the skylight again—
the harsh staccato of tough beaks on domed plastic,
believing those squares of shine are water pools.
I go outside, slapped by sauna heat, and look up
at a pair and their three young—flapping, defiant.
I always thought it the way of winged things
for fledglings to fly quickly off to their own futures.
But these stand together, five black fingers
framed against the heat and smoke-bleached sky.
They glare down at me haughtily
plumage as forbidding as the burned-out mountain,
challenging me to reclaim the covering of my house.

Suddenly, with a raucous cry, they launch
themselves as one into the torrid air.
In a sickle formation of whooshing wings
they propel themselves to nearby oaks,
railing there against another cloudless dusk.
All of us wait for rain.

THE BASHER

Spring, in Virginia, and a splendid scarlet specimen of the state bird persistently flings himself against the window in my home office. Transparent wall of double-paned glass. Thud-flutter, thud-flutter, thud-flutter. I watch as the cardinal perches briefly on the holly tree limb, eyes the lucent expanse, then crashes, wing first. A hundred times that day I wince, the sound echoing everywhere in the house. When it pauses for a minute I run outside, sure I'll find his crumpled carcass on the ground, a limp vermillion sacrifice. This bird proves hardy. What will deter him? I try a Miss March centerfold first, thinking her inflated jugs would frighten any self-respecting bird. He's definitely male—the tempo of his bashing only increases. Teddy bear's button eyes staring through the glass interrupt him for only an hour. I tempt the cats with treats to perch upon the sill but even their hungry green gaze does not dissuade him. Is he trying to fly through the house? Out the other side? All he can see through that window is a blank white wall—and his own reflection. A red-uniformed soldier, he flings himself into resolute battle with an identical enemy. Testosterone poisoning, I think, exasperated. But the next week's bashing cardinal has plumage less vibrant, a smaller, more delicate body, and equal intent to self-destruct.

THE MOVEMENT OF COWS

Sometimes cows migrate
in an orderly fashion
creating a predictable pattern
north to south in the pastures
as the day progresses.
Part of a tranquil scene
as the sun glides from one
mountain range to another
staining the hills and grassland
in patchwork designs.

But there are days when the restless herd
zigzags across dirt roads,
tramps circuitously among
fences and scattered houses,
trailing a bellowing leader,
heads tossing, echoing moos.

An agitated wandering.
Searching for satisfaction
in the next field,
just down the road a piece,
somewhere not quite
within attainable distance.

PLUNGE

Diagnosed—a disease out of nowhere,
I sit in my light-filled kitchen
attempting to choke down some leftovers.
Mental shuffling of internet information,
printed pamphlets, grim pronouncements
of the white-coated ones, all about a treatment
that threatens to be more sinister
than what it attempts to cure.

My cat perches on the chair next to me,
staring and purring—to comfort me, I hope,
though more likely lusting after the shrimp
in my pasta. I pull one out to feed her, when
without warning, a writhing, patterned
curlicue plummets from the skylight, bounces once
off the table, then lands at my feet, hissing and coiling.
For a moment, I'm stunned into stillness.
The feline, intrigued, leaps down to investigate.
That thrusts me into motion. I grab the cat and
shut her in safety, punch three numbers on the phone,
then return with a broom
to keep the poisonous one at bay
until summoned officials arrive.

A friend, upon hearing the story, says,
Imagine how the snake felt.
Yes.
Somnolent sun-baking among tall grasses,
snatched by a sharp-beaked creature, which,
chased by a smaller bird, screeches, loses grip.
The fall to the roof below, seeking escape
the slither to a clear dome,
a baby snake-sized hole in its side.
The wriggle through,
the plunge
into yet another fray.

BATTLES IN THE NIGHT

The tick, tick of tiny insects
trapped between screen and night-closed window,
a minute struggle of almost unseen things.
Bits of translucent wings, fine moth powder
litter the sills in the morning
remnants of an unwitnessed war.

I put the house to bed
each night, make the rounds,
lights extinguished,
cats curled up in accustomed places.
Finally, I fight to dislodge praying mantis,
moths, unidentified desert flyers
from their frantic hold on window screens.

Lured there by our lamps,
radar confused, false day invading
dark promise of the night
insects gather, cling, fling themselves
against the fine-meshed metal.
I pluck and bash against the screen
to no avail, they will not leave.
The closing of the casements
becomes the lowering of coffin lids.

I drift to the darkened bedroom,
prepare to face my own night
battling in dreams, while in other rooms
the futility of window warfare
engages.

WOMAN AND DOG

One morning, as my dog and I ambled
down the long dirt road on the daily quest for news delivery,
the dog's eyes were bright as she snuffled the sun-warmed grass.
She pulled with impatience at the restraint of leash,
leaped with maddened joy when I called her name.

I showered, refreshed by the lukewarm trickle,
pulled on the light, loose clothing
the temperature of the day demanded,
noted with satisfaction the ease with which
the pants slipped over hips—another small victory
over pounds that accompany age.
I felt freedom in the light fabric's swirl,
reminiscent of youthful hippie days.

As I drove the familiar road to work
my eyes were drawn by an old woman, old dog,
struggling through the roadside weeds
to the growling accompaniment of commuter traffic.
The woman was dressed in white cotton that matched
the sparse hair straggling from the sagging brim of her hat,
her body bent into a painful question mark.
She shuffled through the dust and tattered grass
pulling along a reluctant cotton puff of an ancient dog
by a scarlet umbilical cord of leash.
Swept on by the flow of traffic,
I turned away from evidence
in the rearview mirror.

FLAT WORLD

She perceives the world as flat.
To her dulled eyes, dimension is illusion.
White sheets of clouds
are ironed flush against the sky.
The road ahead is even and tedious,
unrolling along the endless beige of plains.

By rote, she pulls herself from her solitary bed,
casts on drab clothing,
forces nourishment into her mouth
and leaves for another bland day.
Arrives unnoticed at the work place,
sits in front of a humming machine
creating messages others will fling
unread to desktops.

In the lunchroom, she listens vaguely
to the stories of spouses, kids, dogs, their antics.
Her mouth wraps itself around a sandwich,
her voice rarely mingles with the others.
She smiles faintly at appropriate times.

In her apartment, she sits and studies
the unadorned white space.
Listens to lives of others through walls.
Walks sometimes to the bathroom,
opens a drawer, rattles blue pills in a bottle,
listens to their call.
Would anyone know the difference?

SINISTER MOON

The awful eye of moon glares from whitened sky,
permeates bedroom blinds, penetrates dreams,
tosses me in my bed.

Swallows mutter from their back porch nest,
bury heads under their wings.
The owl, gliding joyfully over his domain,
knows scurrying prey cannot conceal itself.
Coyotes yelp their hunters' symphony,
while rabbits tremble in illuminated brush.

A once benevolent night transformed
by unrelenting light.

WARD OFF THE NIGHT

Every evening, as night siphons
the fuchsia from the clouds,
the cobalt from the sky,
our dog begins to bark—
a gruff and panicked sound,
more urgent than at any other time of day.
I wonder if she's
summoning the haunting response
of her coyote cousins,
or protesting the ominous
fading of the light.

Every evening, as darkness
wraps her shawl around our houses
humans huddle around plates
of warm, comforting food.
We recite our days
with bursts of laughter,
cluster in front of the
television's artificial brightness,
build fires in brick or metal boxes,
flick switches to summon what light we can.
Do our best
to ward off the night.

OUR WILDERNESS

Seven small-town New Jersey cousins ventured
into our wilderness, in reality, about one square mile
of deeply ravined woodland, where no one
on the outskirts of Trenton could manage to perch a house.
It belonged to some obscure religious group which had erected
crude wooden buildings on the woods' edge
and left the rest untouched, but we considered it ours,
since they were usually rolling holy elsewhere.

We'd wander from the oppressive safety
of our grandparents' too-warm house,
escape from the gathering of grownups,
with their boring anecdotes and watchful eyes,
to become ourselves in the excitement of the forest.
Always something new–a lightning struck tree,
splintered and blackened, a new patch of unearthly plants,
monstrous, soggy piles of leaves, their musty odors
released by the latest deluge, taunting our nostrils.

Enraptured each year by clusters of Jack in the Pulpit,
conjured, we were sure, by the absent religious ones–
hence the name. That delicate flower with its sinister
life's mission, its basin filled with fragrant liquid,
attracting thirsty insects in, then, when they were sated,
ensnaring them within its seductive bowl,
unable to climb the slick walls.
There they remained, slowly digested
by the carnivorous plant.

One of our competitive games was to find
insect victims in the most grotesque state
of partial maceration.
Another was who could run the fastest and farthest
into the darkest part of the woods, where ancient oaks
arched out all trace of sunlight, without scaring ourselves
so badly we'd have to emerge back into the relative safety
of the group. Who could creep closest to the marsh,

without succumbing to the parent-told fable
of the girl who got too close
and was gulped down by quicksand before anyone
could respond to her weakening, pathetic screams.

We all discovered much about ourselves in those years
and that place. Tested our resolve,
our fleetness of foot, our daring,
and our propensity for challenges.
Now, the two youngest of us have gone beyond
memories of that place, or perhaps to where
such memories are all that stay alive.
Those of remaining on the same sphere
as that forest still think
of it with wonder—that time of innocence
in the wilderness
since fled.

LONELY TREES

Each Christmas morning, our family traveled along
New Jersey's snow-lined highways toward the cousins'
houses for our traditional viewing of gifts given and received,
a rite of admiration and envy. Along the familiar roadway,
there were always Christmas tree stands, their duties done,
but not yet packed away. Locked in their board and wire cages
were bedraggled pines and cedars—the unchosen ones.
I saw them as the loneliest trees—unadorned, unloved
by any family–never to hear the squeals of excited children
or admire themselves bedecked in twinkle lights and tinsel.
Their fate to be hauled off, tossed in some landfill,
their beauty wasted. Slaughtered needlessly–taken
from some dense forest, I imagined, chopped from fragrant
life in hopes of some family's brief admiration.
I'd bring tears to my eyes each year, deploring
the fate of these rejected trees.

My family never knew of my musings—
my younger siblings boisterous on the springy
back seat, my parents, in earlier years, lost in one another.
They'd sit as close as possible on the front seat, nuzzling.
But over the years, my mother slid by inches away
from him, until finally she leaned in silence against
the passenger's door, like a tree propped, forsaken,
against the frigid wire mesh of its enclosure.

My mother towered over my father,
sheltered her children in generous branches.
But each year, her roots clung more tenuously
to eroding earth on our small town's riverbank,
until she toppled into the current, borne away
from him, from all of us.

WHICH WAY?

All my life, maps have lied to me. By the time I wrestle with a map's
infinite folds, turn it upside down and sideways, and locate where I am,
I'm inevitably somewhere else. When it looks like I should be turning left,
according to the wisdom of some minuscule black lines, they don't take
into account which direction I'm currently headed, so I end up more
profoundly lost than before. Maps never warn of detours or road work.
Torturous pieces of paper are ill-equipped to deal with reality.

GPS devices are no better. While there's less room for error,
that's part of the problem. I'll be cruising along, dreaming a poem,
letting soft music entertain my ears, when a metallic voice warns
me of something that will happen in two miles, making me jump,
and stuttering my heart. It doesn't allow for bladder urges or craving
for a snack. I pull off the road and it starts shouting, *Turn around NOW!*
Then I have to push endless buttons to shut it up, usually for good.

We can plan all we want, but there are inevitable
roadblocks, obstacles, and wayfaring we cannot foresee.
I figure the best I can do is keep traveling,
and let the journey take me where it will.

FOUNDRY

Every weekday of his life from age 17
to age 67 my father traipsed
to his job at the pipe foundry
traversed those few blocks
through our small-town version
of ghetto. I remember him
energetic in the mornings, swinging
his old metal lunchbox, maybe whistling
a favorite Rodgers & Hammerstein tune.

Then, after eight hours of trudging,
counting, supervising the loading
of tons of pipe onto flatbeds
plodded homeward, skin begrimed,
shirt soaked in wide stripes
under the arms, across the belly.
He'd leave his work boots
at the side door to the cellar
and head directly to the shower.

I wonder now if I only imagined
a school field trip to the foundry,
all of us kids hard-hatted
watched great vats of molten metal
glowing virulent orange, poured
into molds to make those pipes.
The men shouted over incessant
clanging, filthy beyond
recognition as our fathers, brothers.

Hardly a place for children,
it seems now, but back then
kids were deemed less fragile.
The huge smokestacks of the place
belched sparks at night—captive fireworks.
Ash drifted to smudge clothing on backyard lines.

Inside those acres of metal buildings,
all windows blackened, the entire
population of town's men toiled daily,
their lives expended there.
When they heard of Hell on Sundays,
they nodded in recognition.

Now sometimes while driving,
I'll see a site where large-jawed machines
bring up mouthfuls of earth and rusted metal pipes
destined to be replaced with plastic.
Piles of huge browned bones, like those
of long-buried workers,
lie there, futile.

EDGES

The blood-red sun
extinguished itself in the river
after long hours we'd spent
searching for treasures
to add to his collection.
As we strolled, eyes sifting
the sand for pieces of quartz
hewn into blades and tips,
his voice chipped the pattern
for how I should change.

That voice held edges
keen as the arrowheads.
Its intent to harm as deliberate
as a stone point
bound to a shaft of ash
with strips of doe-hide
from previous prey.

CAVE TOUR

You should have known not to enter the gaping mouth
of that rapacious cave. The cool, damp passages, squeezing
the flesh, clothing whispers, a slithering against rock walls.
A scarlet peony of panic blooms in your chest. Not enough air
to suffice for this chuckling crowd; you are deprived.
Ahead, the maddening cheerfulness of a teenaged guide,
her voice practiced in spiel and tone. Too young
and blonde to know of darkness. You crave to—what?
Careen through the dimly lighted path, your voice
a screaming echo in the cave? Become a bat, at home in this
forbidding place? Deep breathe and calm, get through somehow.

What vaguely remembered terror does your brain perceive?
Some childhood game, thought funny by the others?
A power blackout during the hurricane you survived
as a kid, huddled with extended family on the living room floor
while rain bullied its way under the door, and
candlelight quivered in the caterwauling of wind?
Some nameless darkness from the time before you were,
or anticipating the nothingness of the time
when you leave? You force your eyes straight ahead,
concentrate on exchanging one breath for another, creep
toward sight of sunlight at the end of the narrow path.

MEMORY SCENTS

Olfactory is the sense to which my memory
is most firmly tied.   I recall little about
the furnishings in my grandparents' home,
but will never forget its fragrance of ginger
and pungent moss; my grandmother's baking,
and the latter because the house perched
on the edge of a densely wooded ravine.

The home of my other grandparents was redolent
of tobacco smoke, oregano, and simmered garlic,
thanks to my affectionate grandfather's unfiltered
Camels and my aunt's Italian heritage. For decades,
the reek of cigarette smoke smelled
like unadulterated love to me.

The home where my first husband grew up
had the essence of old world Germany—
sauerbraten, sauerkraut, ameliorated
with the ever-present cinnamon kuchen
that beckoned on their kitchen table.
Since his parents always viewed me with skepticism,
to this day, those scents repel me.

The house I later shared with that husband
held the odor of old rugs tinged
with ancient dog, even after we eliminated
all the carpet in the house. New paint odors recalled
the migraines I experienced while redecorating.
Later, as the marriage soured, the rooms
always retained an acrid scent.

My first single apartment reeked
of roach spray and heated arguments
of my neighbors. No matter how I attempted
to brighten the ambience, I knew I needed
to escape from that place before too many
months had passed.

My next apartment, where I grew into
my true self, and realized I could be content
on my own, contained only pleasant fragrances
that I created—soft vanilla, leather
upholstery, the paper that I used in my typed
creativity. Greenery added to the cherished aroma.

There have been many memorable homes since then,
but my current one has equal scents of contentment—
even the faint traces, no matter how much we clean,
of our beloved pets. We create our own fragrances
with all that we cook, and the adventures we live.
It's redolent of happy home to me.

NEW JERSEY BEACH

Burdened like camels, we struggled over the dunes.
Once freed, we kids scampered toward
our fort of dreams, the spot
where concrete ruins lay, mysterious,
their faded mosaics uncovered, recovered
by restless waves and shifting sands,
writing another chapter in our imagined
      histories.

As the sun was hoisted higher in the sky,
we'd cool our feet by squishing them into
the wave-washed sand, coquinas digging
all around, but finding no path through flesh and bone.
Beside us, the pummeled pilings stood, but shuddered
foretelling their eventual
      fall.

Up on drier sand, where the grownups spread
their blankets, robes draped the back of beach chairs
like discarded skins, flesh soaked in baby oil
roasted in the sun, an occasional comment flew
between them like a startled sandpiper.
Our fathers' fierce noses jutted to the sky,
but somehow never burned as red as our small ones.
The bellies of our mothers rounded
higher with the passing of each summer.
Sometimes their hands would caress that new flesh
      wonderingly.

When the afternoon light slanted golden,
and blue melted into horizon's blue
they'd call us, their voices as plaintive
as those of the circling gulls.
We'd take up our burdens once again,
shuffle on salt-stiffened legs
across sands that each day seemed
so much hotter than before,

searing skin on the soles of our feet.
Back to where the sun-battered faces
of houses stood behind their shallow
shields of dune,
    waiting.

NERVOUS

Something large and grey loomed
from the closet, or the skritching
of mouse claws was audible in the walls,
and I scrambled down the narrow stairs
on small, icy feet.
I burst into your room, piping,
Mommy, I can't sleep
I'm too nervous.
You untangled your long tanned legs
from Dad's and sat up, uncovered breasts
swinging toward me, their nipples
like two more dark, accusing eyes.
You rubbed your face awake and
told me, grumpily,
that I was too young to be nervous.

At times of tension in my life
those words of yours reechoed.
I'd wonder if I was old enough yet.
What age it took, exactly,
what round number before
nervousness was permitted.

Since you left without warning,
and I became the family's oldest woman
I've begun to feel
unbuffered in the world.
I see with new interpretation
the fading of my hair,
the flesh that no longer
molds so gracefully to bone.
and I try to believe that
I'm too young to be nervous.

SEARCHING FOR CASTLES

From foreign maps we choose
the tiniest, weaving lines to follow
in our rented car. The roads
barely traced in grey that meander
along blue lines of minor rivers,
and lead to villages with names in
scarcely discernable print.
I tell you, that day,
our mission is a quest for castles,
monuments to some feudal lord's power
where he could observe from his tower
as serfs struggled below in rocky fields.

We speed by vistas of startling green,
the fields are never this emerald-bright at home.
Breezes redolent of centuries of manure
waft in through our open windows.
We seem to be the only car.
People we pass, on foot or bicycle
raise startled hands in greeting,
stare after our bumper, wonderingly.

I point on the map to the castle symbol,
a small cross topped with a battlement flag.
Here. There should be a castle right here.
You screech the brakes and we emerge, shade
eyes from the glare, look over the open field
at nothing, a tree or two scattered,
as if tossed there, carelessly, by a giant's hand,
in the distance a small heap of tumbled stones.
Can that be all that's left?

As shadows crawl across the road
we arrive at a village with
a stern, stone square,
a small hotel.
We struggle, in language barely remembered

from musty high school classrooms
to engage a room from the smirking hotelier,
eat dinner, according to custom, very late.

All night, as the town youths
roar by on their mopeds,
I dream of men in rough brown tunics,
picks and hoes in hand,
battering at great stone walls.

LANDINGS

In the last minutes before landing—at first
it seems like effortless gliding. The engines hush
as the plane sails calmly toward its destination.
Then comes the annoying ping! as the pilot announces
final approach. Soon after, the wheels clunk down
and the enormous winged machine loses its
already delicate balance in the insubstantial air.

As it lumbers toward the runway, there are enemies
in the atmosphere—turbulence bestowed by
cloud layers, thermals produced by
the surrounding mountains. The plane
lurches from side to side, a drunken bear.
Elevates, then thunks down on air pockets.
I grip the arms of my seat, murmur an agnostic's prayer
while my husband, the seasoned jet mechanic, dozes on
or continues nonchalantly to flip the pages
of the airline's magazine.

Finally, after endless tilting to the left, then right
those wheels approach contact with the tarmac.
Most pilots seem to specialize in slamming that bad boy
on the ground, to a great creaking of joints and shifting
of luggage in overhead bins. The P.A. crackles into life
as the attendant welcomes us to our destination,
wishes us a pleasant stay. My husband grins and says,
Well, we beat the odds again. Home again,
home again. And I wish
I could grow similar insouciance
for all of my landings.

Leslie Clark has written for most of her life. She began sending her work out for publication over thirty-five years ago. After some success in having poetry and short fiction published, writing took on an increasing importance in her life, and she resolved to find ways to support and encourage other writers. While Leslie taught in Newport News Public Schools, she founded two programs for young writers. She also founded Isle of Wight Writers' Group in Smithfield, VA after moving there in 1988. Leslie earned her M.A. in English through the creative writing program at Old Dominion University in 1991.

Once Leslie and her husband, Gary, moved to Arizona, she continued activities for the benefit of writers. She taught creative writing and other English classes at Cochise College and co-founded High Desert Writers' Association. In March, 1999, the first Cochise Community Creative Writing Celebration was held at Cochise College. Leslie coordinated the committee which initiated and organized this event, and continued to head the committee until she retired in 2013.

Leslie's poetry and fiction have been published in such journals as *Bogg, Impetus, The Poet's Domain, Legacy Arts, Cedar Rock* and many others. Finishing Line Press published her poetry chapbook *Cardiac Alert* in 2009. Leslie established a quarterly online poetry journal, *Voices on the Wind* http://voicesonthewind.net in 2005, and continues to publish poets from all over the U.S.

In 2017, Leslie and her husband and their rescue pets moved to Oceanside, California to be in proximity to the beautiful Pacific Ocean. In Oceanside, she founded and moderates a new writers' group at the Mission Branch of the public library.

www.ingramcontent.com/pod-product-compliance
Lightning Source LLC
LaVergne TN
LVHW021125080426
835510LV00021B/3324